LAYERS OF INK

A JOURNEY THROUGH WORDS, WOUNDS AND WONDER

DR. SARVANI

Made with ♥ on the Notion Press Platform
www.notionpress.com

To my **Appa**,

who filled my world with books and quietly lit the spark to write.

To my **Amma,**

who saw beauty in my words before I ever did,

and cheered every line I dared to share.

To my **Husband**,

who healed me with love,

and gave me the freedom to be entirely, unapologetically me.

To my **Sister,**

my constant sounding board,

whose creativity and care brought these pages to life.

To my **In-laws**,

for your constant encouragement and belief in my journey.

Thank you—for being my home, my strength, and my story.

Contents

Preface

Author's Preface

I'm Dr. Sarvani, a pathologist by profession and a poet at heart.

Writing poetry has been my refuge and companion since childhood — a quiet dream I've carried through the years.

For me, poetry is more than just words; it's a way to feel, to reflect, and to heal.

This book is a deeply personal collection rooted in emotions, self-awareness, and the unspoken poetry of everyday life.

In a world that moves fast, I chose to pause — to observe, to feel, and to write.

To challenge myself and grow as a writer, I embraced various poetry challenges:
poems without certain letters, reflections written backward, storytelling through verse, and more.
Each piece stretched my creativity while remaining grounded in authenticity.

Some poems were refined using digital tools to help me express myself more clearly — but every thought, every feeling, every story began with me.
This is my voice, shaped by experience, emotion, and intention.

Thank you for reading.
I hope these pages offer you comfort, connection, and maybe even the courage to write your own truths.

— *Dr. Sarvani*

@books_bakers

Acknowledgements

Every layer of ink on these pages rests on the quiet strength of others.

First, to my parents—**Appa and Amma**—for filling my childhood with books, markets, and the simple courage to feel deeply. Appa, your love of language still lights my way; Amma, your unflagging faith in my words made this book inevitable.

To my husband, **Ritesh**, who healed what hurt and insisted I remain "me" in every sentence. Your steady presence is the margin that keeps my lines in place.

To my sister, **Sindhoosha**, designer of late-night layouts and early-morning pep talks—thank you for turning my scattered drafts into something beautiful.

To my **In-laws**, for patiently helping me select and refine the book cover designs and interiors. Your care and attention made this journey even more beautiful.

Heart-felt thanks to **Notion Press** for their intuitive online tools and publishing support—your platform turned possibility into print. To the silent community on Instagram **@books_bakers**—each like, comment, and DM reminded me that poetry still finds its people.

My **Pathologist colleagues** at the lab, who tolerated my random lines and talks on poems and books: thank you for believing that science and art can coexist.

Finally, to **every reader** now holding this book: you grant these poems a second heartbeat. May they return the favour in quiet moments of your own.

— Dr. Sarvani

Prologue

Why I Write

Amidst the chaos,
Writing is where I find my solace.
    Having chaos around ignites
The mind to vent out the sufferings.
    Writing gives the comfort
For life which has been confused and incomplete.
    Finding the little joys in the write-ups
Makes me happy and completes my day.

— by Dr. Sarvani

1. Inner Worlds & Emotional Echoes

Inner Worlds & Emotional Echoes

These poems are quiet conversations with the self —
where emotion is raw, reflection is necessary, and healing begins.

In this section, I navigate fear, grief, anger,
and the quiet ache of acceptance.
These aren't just feelings —
they're echoes of moments that demanded to be felt,
understood, and transformed.

May these verses offer you a mirror
to see your own resilience,
and a reminder that even our most private battles
carry the seeds of light.

The Whole You – Layers of Survival

I never really knew the issue inside me,
to talk about it was a distant dream.

It has been buried deep,
buried beneath layers of scar tissue,
each one a silent story of survival.

I deny my emotions to everyone,
I never learned to feel them,
as feeling them would make me weak,
I never took that break.

I knew pent-up emotions may tear me asunder,
but can I gather the shards of my soul?

Accepting emotions is a step towards healing,
recognizing the mind's turmoil—its value, its power—
knowing that every piece of me matters.

Fear

Deeply rooted, never fleeting,
Born from ashes, chaos breeding.

Tethered to the past,
Present moments slipping fast.
Forgetting isn't an option,
Fighting isn't simple.

Childhood wounds might be the source,
Toxic ties could set the course.
Positive words might heal,
Or therapy to break the seal.

Dwelling on the past won't free you,
Craft the present to renew.
Let go of haunted thoughts,
Rewrite them in golden scripts.
Rise and fight,
Fear isn't right.

Grief

Drowning in the sea of tears,
I grieve and lose my way.

No hope, no light, no end in sight,
I struggle every day.
I try to breathe,
I try to cope,
I try to move ahead.

But peace eludes me in this storm,
I feel the weight of dread.

Will I ever see the shore, where happiness awaits?
Will I ever break the waves, that keep me in this state?

I hope this pain will make me strong,
and teach me how to heal.
I hope this phase will pass along,
and show me how to feel.

Time is what I need the most,
to mend my broken heart.
Change is what I seek the most,
to make a fresh new start.

Away from this dark ocean,

I sail with zeal and hope—

Towards the mountains of beauty,

I climb with faith and scope.

The Mirror I Feared

The mirror saw what I tried to hide—
Marked by deep scars across bare skin.

Each glance, a quiet ache,
A memory etched in flesh.

You cloaked my thoughts in borrowed light,
But what remained were shreds of pain.

You made me lose my confidence, my power,
Made me face the sharp truth of failure.

It hurt to meet you eye to eye,
But I had no choice—
And so I stayed,
Caressed the scars,
And healing began from within.

Flaw by flaw, I began to see:
I love you.

Stepping out from shadow,
You stood strong—
Letting me shine even in darkness.

I love you for who you are.
I love the reflection I see.

Empowered, accepted, and free—
I love you, myself.

Anger

It all takes few seconds to think and talk,
But I never made that walk.

I regret said words and cry,
But never succeeded the try.

I fail to control my tongue,
With which I lose my league.

Perhaps with effort, I'll find serenity,
A soothing balm for my tempest's intensity.

Anger must be shed, replaced,
With calm thoughtfulness embraced.

I pray for patience from above,
To test my essence, my sense of love.

For controlling anger is a patient art,
A journey of the soul,
a mastery of the heart.

Forgiveness

In quiet bus rides, I reflect
On journeys past, and weights I've checked.

Toxic relationships, once a burden bore —
Now scars remain, but spirits soar.

Embracing healed wounds, I move ahead,
Loving family, safe relationships spread.

Strength forged in fire, I now unfold,
Unshackling chains of yesterday's gold.

Was it the darkness that made me strong?
Or the courage to release the weight so long?

Forgiveness, a liberating power,
Unburdens me from each passing hour.

With every step, I rise anew —
Freedom from fears, handcuffs broken through.

Pathway to a whole new me unfolds,
Unleashing strength, young and bold.

Forgiveness, a gift I give to myself,
Unshackling the past, I find my wealth —

In the freedom to love, to live, to be —
A whole new me, wild and carefree.

2. Longing, Love & Loss

Longing, Love & Loss

Love doesn't always announce itself with warmth.

Sometimes, it arrives as an ache,

a silence,

or the space someone leaves behind.

These poems speak to the unsent letters,

the unspoken words,

the quiet grieving of those we loved, lost,

or never truly reached.

In these pages, I explore the tender terrain of memory and

heartache —

where longing lingers,

and healing begins in whispers.

The Unsent Letter

If I had the courage to write to you,
I would've asked where I stood in your heart.
I would've asked for closure.
I would've whispered the love I hid so well.

I would've longed for bliss, for your touch.
To soak in love,
To fly away with you,
To drown in ecstasy.

I would've spent my nights wrapped in longing,
Woken to mornings made of soft light and deeper truth.
I would've torn away the superficial,
To make it raw, real, and ours.

But now I see —
I am happier than I ever was.
I've found what I once only dreamed of.

You were the end
That led me to a truer beginning.

Thank you — A passing cloud
That cleared my skies, for real love.

The Contrasts

There's a place where light meets the shadows —
Where the glow of your thoughts touches
The darkest corners of my life,
Unveiling secrets long buried,
Pinning my soul to old pain,
Filling my present with echoes of the past.

There's a place where silence swallows the noise —
Your quiet soul deafens me
With the storm of questions in my mind.
What went wrong to deserve this silence?
It steals my strength,
Leaves me bare, vulnerable, undone.

There's a place where the contrasts meet and merge —
Where differences don't divide, but desire.
They twist together,
Colliding in love,
Unravelling in lust.

Without Saying It

The path to you is both my journey and destination,
The long-awaited smile at the end of each day.

Your laughter brings light to my darkest moments,
And with your joy, mine multiplies in every way.

You are the piece I've searched for through time,
The one with whom I can simply be.
You understand the silence of my heart,
And in your presence, I am free.

You take my hand through uncertain streets,
Where doubt and fear might try to sway.
You carry my name close to your chest,
As if my life were your gift each day.

With you, I grow, unfold, and stray —
Into freedom, into bloom, into my own way.

You are the one my soul has yearned for,
The one who stirs the stillness inside.
You're the spark that makes butterflies dance,
The dream I no longer need to hide.

It's for You, DAD - *The Space You Left*

It's just the void —
a hollow nothingness that won't be filled.

A silent gap in the air,
your space, Dad —
unfiltered, unattended,
aching in its absence.

Every day,
I carry the weight of not being there,
not holding your hand in the final moments.

I miss the quiet,
the long talks,
the simple walks,
the way your presence made the world feel steady.

Now, it's just the space left behind.
Just me —
confused,
shattered,
searching for a way to understand.

I miss you, Dad.
In every step I take,

in every breath,

in every moment I wish I could share with you.

I owe you everything.

I am grateful.

I love you.

I love you.

Rest in peace, Dad.

I'm sorry.

3. Identity, Memory & Growth

Identity, Memory & Growth

In these poems, I return to the roots
of who I've been
and who I'm becoming.

Through childhood memories, forgotten passions,
and quiet self-reflection,
this section explores the tender space between past and present —
between the girl I was
and the woman I continue to grow into.

Here, memory becomes a compass,
and growth,
a quiet act of courage.

Growing up..

I knew a girl with fire in her eyes,
Bold in her steps, chasing the skies.

She spoke her truth, wrote songs with ease,
Danced through life like a gentle breeze.

She questioned rules that made no sense,
Fought her fears with confidence.

A dreamer with a fearless soul,
Living life, completely whole.

But time, as always, had its say,
And slowly, life got in the way.

The poems paused, the voice grew still,
Doubt crept in, replaced the will.

Now I stand — quiet, unsure,
A softer heart, a little obscure.

Yet in the echoes of my past,
I hear her laughter — free, steadfast.

She never left — just lost in time,
Buried beneath routine and rhyme.

So here I am, with open heart,
Ready again to play her part.

To grow is not to lose our flame,
But to return to it — not the same.

Wiser now, with gentler might,
Still bold enough to chase the light.

Childhood Memory

Holding my father's hand,
I strolled down the market lane,
Amid the hustle and bustle of life.

Vendors, their wares displayed,
And a tight grip on Amma's list,
Curious eyes met fresh veggies,
I learned the art of selection.

As my appa spoke with them,
Negotiating price and quality,
I witnessed the dance of bargaining and buying.

These memories etched within my mind —
Whenever I walk the market lane,
I feel their presence, guiding me through life.

People may come and go, but memories stay,
A compass of love, forever leading the way.

Thank you, Appa and Amma,
for showing me the path.

The Forgotten Rhythm

As I drove into the parking lot,
Anklet sounds filled the temple premises,
Transporting me back to a cassette of past memories,
Where self-reflection stood, patiently waiting.

A decade has passed since I last danced,
Yet nostalgia lingers
as tiny tots sway to the rhythm.

I know the little me scolds from afar,
Chiding me for leaving
such a precious talent behind.

I spoke to my master —
Little has he changed,
Always dressed in black,
His ivory beard a testament to time.

Reality wraps me tightly,
Caught in the infinite rat race,
As hobbies and passions fade away.

Yet life's rhythms spin a vibrant tapestry —
A dance of moments,

melodies to reclaim,

A spark ignites, urging me to revive,

To embrace the art,

and dance once again.

Between Two Worlds - *Millennial reflection on screens, nature & disconnection*

My neck screams in agony,
my shoulders too,
From endless scrolling on screens,
my body feels anew.

I yearn to gaze upon nature's splendour and might,
But my brain craves
the instant thrill of digital delight.

Generations have evolved,
yet quality has declined —
Games replaced by phones,
relationships reduced to mere coins.

I never thought I'd be
the bridge between two worlds apart,
Witnessing the transition
from lush jungles to concrete hearts.

It's hard to fill the void,
to reconcile the past and present,
But I'm proud to be a millennial,
with a unique perspective to invent.

4. Creative Challenges & Literary Play

Creative Challenges & Literary Play

This section is where form meets freedom —
where poetry becomes both a puzzle and a playground.

Born from writing prompts and poetic constraints,
these pieces invited me to stretch beyond my comfort zone.

Whether it's a poem without the letter "e,"
an alphabetic journey from A to Z,
or a story told through an unsent letter,
each challenge became a doorway to new expression.

May these poems spark your own curiosity —
and perhaps even your pen.

Narrative Challenge: Missing You the Most, Appa

The beeping of the vitals turned red… then flat.
The nurse said softly, "He's gone… at last."

I came running — too late by far,
Just to see you lying silent, from afar.

Still. Calm.
And as always, wearing the last smile.

COVID took you away from us, Dad,
And we missed you in every way possible.

The chaos rose — you weren't there to calm it.
The stress hit hard — you weren't there to ease it.

And one by one,
It sent us all to the hospital the following day.

Nightmares. Cries.
Ma and sis holding the pillars tight,
While I drowned in tears,
Missing my beloved Dad —
Still trying to understand what goodbye really meant.

The years have passed,
But the pain feels raw…
Like you left us just yesterday.

Your favorite chair still sits by the door,
As if you might walk in once more.

Ma still lights the lamp at night,
Whispering your name into the flickering light.

I still follow your ways —
Your decision-making calm,
Your stress-handling strength,
The way you faced storms like they were passing clouds.

You left me more than memories —
You left me tools.
Ways to breathe,
Ways to be.

You're not here,
But you're never really gone.

You're in my thoughts,
In my breath,
In the calm I try to keep,
In the woman I'm still trying to become.

And in every choice I make,

I ask myself,

"Would Appa be proud?"

Missing you the most, Appa.

Always.

Challenge: No use of the letter "E"

A balcony full of flora
Surrounding aroma
I find light within.

Sitting on rock,
I took a journal along,
Molding thought to word.

Winding up, I found my soul —
Calm, blissful, glad.

Challenge: Reflective Mirror Poem (Palindrome)

Love makes me go crazy,
The way I be.
I be the way,
As if I am crazy in love.

I know this is me,
Crazier and cosier with words.
Words cosier and mind crazier,
Me is the one I know.

Love isn't always special,
To address my whole needs.
Needs to be addressed,
By me isn't love really is — self love.

Thanking the universe,
For the wishes granted.
Granted wishes made me to,
Thank the universe…

Anadiplosis Theme: Finding You

In the quiet of the moment, happiness finds you.
You shine in memories, untouched by time.
Time slips by, but your presence stays.
Stays in the corners of faded dreams.

Dreams where we meet without the world's weight.
Weight of silence speaks what I can't.
Can't forget the nearness we once had.
Had I the chance, I'd hold on longer.

Longer than forever, if such things exist.
Exist in a world where you're far away.
Away from reach, yet close in heart.
Heart still whispers what lips never do.

Do you know, in the quiet of the moment, happiness finds you?

Challenge : A–Z Poem— Alphabetic Journey

Asking the universe to

Be with me,

Counting on it to

Deliver the things I wish for.

Every time I ask

For a favor from

God —

He says it takes time.

I never believed in time,

Just never truly believed myself.

Knowing everything doesn't happen,

Leaving it all in the middle.

Maybe not every

New opportunity

Opens just because we plead.

Perhaps the questions fall on me.

Quietly, I recall

Resilience and strength —

So I answer back,
Tougher this time,
Up and above.

Very bold, the decision ahead —
What's happened till now is my X,
X marks the past,
Yet I need to travel to find my
Zing.

Observational Challenge: Everyday Unknown

The officer, hustling through the papers.
Trip after trips go on the taxi.
The student — drifting through traffic,
a zing in motion.

Pillars held strong by the daily wagers.
The fruit vendor — selling his harvest of love.

The cycle of life goes on.
Despite the differences, people work —
for bed,
for food,
for money.

Spectators of other lives,
while carrying our own fights quietly.

Unnoticed kindness happens in the in-betweens —
a silent nod,
a hand held out,
a smile given without reason.

Not all giving needs to be loud.
We judge, we juggle,

and still we leave room to smile a bit.

Making the day brighter, just a bit —
for others, and for yourself.

Because who really knows
who needs it more?

5. Reflections & Realizations

Reflections & Realizations

These closing poems are moments of pause —
where clarity surfaces, even if briefly,
and the journey begins to make sense.

They reflect what's been felt, faced, and forgiven.
From travel memories to inner reckonings,
this section offers quiet resolutions
and glimpses of peace.

Not endings, but gentle reminders:
you've come a long way,
and you're still unfolding.

Ladaki in Ladakh

Crashing through parting clouds,
Reaching the land of high passes,
Excited for an adventurous bike trip,
I stood at the airport
with my love by my side.

Hopping into the travel car,
Seeing the rocky tar,
Reaching the hotel like a shooting star,
We were left for the day.

A total of twelve,
Biking for the first time,
Soaring high with dreams,
We started the journey to explore **Leh**.

Riding through the rocks,
Scorching under the sun,
Crashing down mountains,
We reached the **Sangam**.

Rafting at high altitude,
Beating in unison,
Making waves,

Creating memories.

Eating at the Gurudwara,
Drawn to Magnetic Hill,
Paying respect at the Hall of Fame,
We enjoyed our day in **Leh**.

Dusting all throughout,
Sweating through the gear,
Breathing hard,
We reached **Hunder**.

Walking through the dunes,
Camels humping all along,
Jumping through the route,
We cracked the evening breeze
at the sand dunes.

Singing the national anthem since childhood,
Wishing for the nation's freedom,
Watching enemy fences from afar,
Reviving the chaos through binoculars,
feeling nostalgic.

Riding the longest of the tour,
Having a great ride with
Aching bums and legs,

We survived the day at **Hunder**.

Off-roading is key,
Heading to **Pangong Tso**,
Seeing the lake crystal blue,
Left my eyes in awe.

Clicking pics,
Capturing memories,
Shivering nights,
We spent the trip together.

Chilling weather,
Breaking routes,
Surrounded by rocky mountains,
Riding with trust and love,
Together, a bond of friendship.

6. Your Turn – Poetry Prompts & Pages

Your Turn – Poetry Prompts & Pages

Poetry has been my mirror,

my medicine,

and my map.

Now, I offer you the pen.

This section invites you to explore your own inner landscape —

through prompts inspired by the same challenges

that shaped this book.

Whether you're a seasoned writer or simply curious,

these pages are for your truths,

your voice,

your ink.

There's no right way to write —

only your way.

Begin where you feel most,

and let the words find you.

Write about a powerful emotion (like grief, fear, or anger) - *without naming the emotion itself.*

Write a poem using only phrases you
overheard or read in the past 24 hours

Recall a childhood memory and write it as a
present-moment experience

Create a poem where every line begins with
the next letter of the alphabet (A–Z)

Write a poem on a memory set in one season

Craft an unsent letter to someone who changed your life but doesn't know it.

Write a poem using no words with the letter
"e."

Explore a lost hobby — and what it meant to
you then, and now.

Write a poem that tells a true story from your life, start to finish.

Describe someone you love — *without ever using the word "love."*

Retell a favourite myth in your own poetic
style.

Write a poem that uses repetition (anaphora or anadiplosis) to build emotional rhythm

Compose a single-sentence poem without any
punctuation marks

Write a mirror poem (start and end with the
same line, or make it symmetrical in structure)

Describe a moment of forgiveness — of yourself or someone else — without using the word "sorry."

Write a travel poem — not about a place, but about who you became because of it.

A Last Word

Thank you for walking these pages with me.

Every poem lives twice—once when it is written,

and again when it is read.

You have given these words their second life.

If something here lingered in your heart,

I hope you'll let it lead you to your own ink.

May your stories find their voice,

your silences find their sound,

and your courage find the page.

Share Your Reflections

• Leave a review on **Instagram**, **Amazon** (it helps other readers find these poems).

• Rate or discuss the book on **Goodreads.**

Every word of feedback keeps poetry alive.

Stay Connected

Find me on **Instagram @books_bakers** & drop a note. I'd love to hear what blooms for you.

Until our lines cross again,

may your days be layered with wonder.

— *Dr. Sarvani*

@books_bakers